Notes / E

Gay Steam: True Sex Tales From The Tubs

PUBLISHED BY: Bathhouse Blues

I have tried to recreate events, locales, and conversations from my memories of them. To maintain their anonymity, in some instances, I have changed the names of individuals and places; I may have changed some identifying characteristics and details such as physical properties, occupations, and places of residence.

PRAISE FOR BATHHOUSE BLUES

"This anonymous web author's essays are worth a browse. Be advised that it's all straight-talking expository dialogue, earnest and in some cases, a bit wide-eyed. Still, the author's intentions are noble." - Unzipped Magazine

"What a good effort here to educate and enlighten people on an area that is little known by outsiders - the gay bathhouse. Recommended." - Jane's Guide

"Bathhouse Blues is the best thing I've read about the sexual politics of gay sex in a semi-public arena." - Tablet Magazine

"These stories may not get you off, but they provide a fascinating characterization of a system that many gay men draw themselves into without really knowing why." - Dark Post

"Well written and entertaining site packed with exciting stories and information, whether you are a bathhouse regular, or have always wondered what goes on in these places. The author delves into pretty much every topic you can imagine about the tubs." - Search The Gay Web

MORE TITLES BY THIS AUTHOR

Bathhouse Blues
Your Guide To Gay Bathhouses

No Asians Please
How Asian Men Are Perceived In The Gay Community

Back To The Baths
More Gay Bathhouse Stories

The Gay Men's Guide To Glory Holes
What Every Man, Gay Or Straight, Needs To Know About Glory Holes

TABLE OF CONTENTS

INTRODUCTION

From the author of Bathhouse Blues come real-life sex tales originating from the gay baths. Gay Steam features stories of actual gay sex encounters at the tubs. Every story in this book is based on my personal observations.

I have written and maintained the website Bathhouse Blues for over 20 years. This site gives readers a peek at what goes on inside a gay bathhouse. Even after two decades, Bathhouse Blues is the only source for gay men to learn about the politics and etiquette of bathhouse culture.

For many years, readers have asked me to write more erotic and steamy stories—man-on-man action. The problem is that I don't have many tales to tell. As faithful fans know, I don't get lucky at the baths.

However, I have observed my share of hot hookups over the years, with so much gay sex happening out in the open. Bookshelves are replete with a plethora of gay erotic stories set in the baths. However, the majority of these stories have undergone fictionalization. That's what makes the book Gay Steam so unique. Everything is 100% true, as all these stories have actually happened in a gay bathhouse setting.

Keep that in mind as you immerse yourself in these captivating stories. Get undressed, wrap a towel around your waist, and venture into the world of the gay baths. It will be a visit you will never forget. Thanks for reading. Me.

Chapter 1
A View From The Rear

I was about to exit my room when I saw a skinny Asian guy rush by my door. I watched as he hurriedly walked down the hall, naked, his ass swinging back and forth while clutching some condoms. He was definitely in a hurry.

Hmmm, I wondered. I guess someone is going to get very lucky. Perhaps Mr. Skinny Asian, in his nude state, is preparing himself. Maybe he was in the middle of something. As I walked around, I began to hear heavy moans and groans. Someone is getting pounded up the ass. It must be Mr. Skinny Asian, whom I saw moments ago with the condoms. The moans were becoming increasingly loud, and it appeared that he was receiving pleasure from the experience. I wondered if he was the top or the bottom in this encounter. The loud groans of ecstasy I heard made it difficult to determine his position. A precise beat accompanied the groans of "AHHHHH!" I heard the same sound over and over. The pounding was swift and precise.

Whoever was bottoming, his groaning continued unabated.

I made my way through the maze of rooms, trying to find—by sound—where the noise came from. The noise of the fucking was becoming increasingly loud, making it simple to locate the source. Finally, I found the room where the fuck was taking place, and someone was already eavesdropping outside the door. Hearing two men engage in sexual intercourse is equally captivating as witnessing it in person.

Are you ready for a bit of irony? One frequent visitor to the bathhouse occupied a room directly across the hall from the location of the noisy altercation. This bathhouse regular was lying face down, his ass exposed, but he had turned his head to see who was passing by. He was eagerly anticipating a sexual encounter. But no one was interested. This is Mr. Bathhouse's typical routine: ass up for hours, waiting for someone to fuck him. However, directly across the hallway, another individual was experiencing the most incredible fuck of his life. Mr. Bathhouse's hole belonged in the Petrified Forest.

Meanwhile, a crowd began to gather in the hallway, listening to the relentless pounding of someone's ass. I heard the shrieks of AHHHHH! It felt like a never-ending cyclical loop. For me, it wasn't about the sex. It was more about being curious about who paired up with whom, observing the aesthetics of their relationship, and understanding how certain duos ultimately end up together. The appearance and dominance of these two intrigued me.

Suddenly the door flew open. I thought, 'Let's see what this duo looks like.' When I peered in the doorway, I wasn't surprised. Mr. Muscle Man was giving Mr. Skinny Asian a severe pounding. Mr. Muscle Man slammed Mr. Skinny Asian, who was lying along the length of the bed with his legs up. Indeed, it was a sight to behold. Even Mr. Bathhouse from the room across the hall was curious and stood up to have a look.

Leaving the door open for everyone to see signifies the occupant's desire for attention. Soon, men began to gather around the doorway, eager to witness the action unfold. I found the sexual attraction between these two incredibly fascinating. You would think Mr. Muscle Man would be interested in the person across the hall. They were similar in age and body type. Instead, he paired up with this skinny Asian twink. Perhaps he simply finds men with impressive asses appealing. Asian men are renowned for having a lovely bubble butt.

The crowd began to disperse, even as the pounding continued for all to see. Mr. Muscle Man then changed positions. He lifted Mr. Skinny Asian and placed him doggy style on the length of the bed. Then he continued with the pounding. Simultaneously, Mr. Skinny Asian could be heard repeatedly shrieking, "AHHHH!" Neither seemed tired, as they had passed the 30-minute mark of this marathon.

Suddenly, Mr. Muscle Man pushed Mr. Skinny Asian down, laying him face first, flat on the bed. Mr. Muscle Man forcefully positioned himself on top of Mr. Skinny Asian and continued to pound with intensity. He synchronized his movements with the exclamations of AHHHHH! His butt cheeks were gyrating to the beat of AHHHHH! Mr. Muscle Man persisted in giving him intense pleasure as he took the hands of Mr. Skinny Asian and held them tightly. One thing that I noticed was a lack of warmth between these two. The fuck session was cold and mechanical. This couple lacked any emotion—no kissing, no touching, and no caressing. Mr. Skinny Asian craved affection from a white man and opened his hole to get it. However Mr. Muscle Man's sole desire was to pound a loose hole, so he wasn't interested in getting close.

I wanted to see the face of Mr. Skinny Asian, but one middle-aged guy positioned his body right in front of me, so it was difficult to see. Pardon the pun, but the middle-aged guy was an asshole for doing that. Bathhouse etiquette tip: if someone leaves their door open for others to watch a fuck, show generosity by sharing the space for everyone to see. It is selfish to block the views of others by being the only one able to watch.

Then, just as suddenly as the door had opened, it had quickly shut. I couldn't determine who shut the door—Mr. Muscle Man or the middle-aged guy. This observation led me to speculate that Mr. Skinny Asian and the middle-aged man might have been friends. Someone is exerting effort to safeguard the privacy of this couple.

Whatever the case, I walked back to my room, shut the door, and lay on the bed. I couldn't help but wonder when I would be lucky enough to have such a fantastic fuck like that.

Chapter 2
No Takers For Gangbang

I first noticed him upon entering the baths at 9:30 that morning. He was a redheaded twink loitering outside a room. I didn't give him a second thought as I prepared for my stay at the baths.

Later on, I noticed him walking around with a significantly older man. I suspected he must be turning tricks. My observation was based strictly on the vast age difference between the two. My thinking was Mr. Redhead is likely heterosexual, engaging in gay sex work, and came here to meet a client.

Sometime later, I went upstairs to the outdoor patio on the roof. Then I noticed Mr. Redhead and an older man walking in together. As I continued to work on my laptop, Mr. Redhead took a seat directly across from me on a couch. The older fellow said he felt cold and expressed his desire to return inside. Mr. Redhead and I were the only ones present as he gazed at me and stroked his cock.

I continued using my laptop, assuming he wouldn't be interested in me. Then a furry forty-year-old guy appeared and seemed quite taken by Mr. Redhead. He was ecstatic to see him all alone. The furry guy swooped down on him, sucking off his twinkly cock. It was difficult not to watch, but I would rather not be rude by staring. Guys often get close up to watch males fuck at the baths. When I say "close-up," we are talking nose-to-nose close, which is just bad manners. The proper etiquette is to watch from a distance. An invitation, like a nod or wink, is required if you want to join in.

During a pause in the sucking, Mr. Redhead looked me straight in the eyes and said to me, "I know you want it." His crotch was the "it" item in question; it was not erect but rather soft. The limpness of his dick was probably due to party drugs. Many narcotics cause erection problems, hence the term "meth cock." Or perhaps his cock had become fatigued due to the intense activity it underwent. I excused myself by saying, "Thanks, but no thanks." Who knew how many raw asses that cock had been in? He'd been at the baths since before 9:30 AM, and it was now 3 PM. But that was not the main reason for my disinterest. Sucking off some random person, no matter how beautiful they are, doesn't do anything for me.

I assumed he wasn't the kind of person to consistently face rejection, particularly from an Asian guy like me. Aren't all Asian guys expected to pursue sex with white men? But not all Asians fit that stereotype. Meanwhile, Mr. Redhead was growing bored with Mr. Hairy. All Mr. Hairy wanted to do was suck, but Mr. Redhead didn't reciprocate. Instead, Mr. Redhead flipped him over and tried to fuck him without a condom. Mr. Hairy, sensing the inappropriateness of this behavior, abruptly stopped it. Soon afterward, they both got up and exited the patio. I continued to type away on my laptop, thinking Mr. Redhead was probably straight, a gay-for-pay hustler. However, I have been wrong before.

Later, I put my laptop away and headed out to walk the halls in search of some action. As I entered the Dungeon Room, the sling area was bustling with activity. A man lay in a sling, relishing the pleasure of being barebacked. Very commonplace. Upon closer inspection, it was Mr. Redhead bottoming and Mr. Hairy topping! Mr. Redhead was gaining popularity as the number of men watching grew. But Mr. Redhead's timing was off. He picked the incorrect time for a gangbang. It was 3 PM, not 3 AM. The early morning hours tend to attract more sexually high, alcohol- and drug-fueled men who are eager to get off. The afternoons only have nervous Nellies walking around.

Despite Mr. Hairy's persistent pounding and Mr. Redhead's continued submission, no one appeared to be willing to take the lead. Mr. Hairy withdrew his cock and surveyed the area to determine whether anyone desired to continue fucking Mr. Redhead. But there were no takers. The group of men were merely pleasuring themselves without any intention of taking control.

Mr. Redhead transitioned from the sling to the saddle stacker and got into position. He likely reasoned that this new position would pose less of a threat to the crowd. Mr. Redhead lay face down, anticipating the arrival of cocks to fill his brightly pink hole. Once again, it was solely Mr. Furry who initiated the action, with everyone else simply observing. Mr. Furry would start and stop, looking around to see if anyone wanted to alternate as a top for Mr. Redhead. There were no takers. At one point, someone fingered him, and Mr. Redhead took offense and shooed him away. Eventually, an East Asian man stepped forward and began to pump. But Mr. Redhead didn't like his technique and stopped it. He slid off the saddle stacker and walked out, followed by Mr. Hairy.

As Mr. Redhead walked through the halls, Mr. Hairy faithfully followed him. A gaggle of guys, all hot for Mr. Redhead, followed in turn. These men wanted Mr. Redhead but didn't want to fuck him. Everywhere Mr. Redhead went, this crowd followed. At one point, an in-shape Asian guy cornered him and started to worship his body. As the Asian began to suck his nipples, Mr. Redhead quickly brushed him aside. Mr. Redhead wanted a hard fuck, not sweet lovemaking.

Mr. Redhead continued to walk down different hallways and knock on doors. Most likely, he was checking to see if the men who fucked him the` previous night were still around. I gave up watching this saga and moved on to something else. The last thing I saw was Mr. Hairy standing outside Mr. Redhead's room, trying to encourage guys to come in for a tag team fuck.

I assumed that Mr. Redhead was under the influence of meth. He probably has a sexual high that needs to be satisfied. Despite his cock being constantly limp, it didn't stop men from repeatedly fucking him in the ass. I wondered if he would be there the next day, and sure enough, he was! This time, an older Black man accompanied him. They were lying on his bed, engaging in conversation. Twinks like Mr. Redhead tend to attach themselves to older men, who are all interchangeable. Yesterday it was Mr. Hairy; today, it is a Black guy.

I got the feeling that the meth was starting to wear off of Mr. Redhead. He wasn't as sexually available as he was the day before. He was more cautious, more selective. I said hello to him several times, but he acted as if I had insulted him. Yep, the drugs were wearing off. He seemed to be back to his old self.

As I left that day, he was hanging out in front of his room. I had last seen him in the same spot two days prior. Some people you see at the baths pique your curiosity about their motivations. I don't need to delve into the motivations of this particular individual, as they seem all the same. This is one curiosity that has been satisfied.

.

Chapter 3
Quick Afternoon Sex

It was a weekday afternoon at the gay baths as I was typing away on my trusted laptop. When I looked up, I saw this white, well-defined guy in his twenties, leaning against the bar, drinking a beer. I thought he was cute, then returned to my work. I did notice that he was standing there completely in the nude. He was not even sporting a towel. Just then, an Asian guy showed up and walked right past Mr. Nude, who checked out the Asian as he passed by.

Things That Make You Go Hmmmm…. But then again, so what? White guys don't dig Asian guys. However, approximately 1% of gay white men do find Asian males attractive, which is a minimal percentage. Maybe this person is in the 1% category. Who knows? But I did notice Mr. Nude glancing my way. Not wanting to be disappointed, I ignored him and continued typing on my laptop. At one point, I needed to use the restroom and walked past Mr. Nude. He didn't even turn his head, so I wasn't a head-turner for him. But I did notice his ass, and what a creamy white thing it was. I also noticed Chinese language tattoos on his body.

That's what irritates me the most. I see men with tattoos of the Chinese language all over their bodies. Yet they want nothing to do with Asian men. I understand that it's possible to appreciate Asian culture without feeling drawn to Asian men. I get that. However, it irritates me only slightly.

Mr. Nude vanished from the bar area sometime during my typing session. Time for a break, I thought. I wandered off to the porn room and found a chair to sit in. I was sitting there not so much to watch porn but to watch the antics that occasionally occur in that area. I was pleasantly surprised when Mr. Nude entered the room. He was leaning against a wall when an Asian man appeared and stood next to him. Here it comes, I thought. I suspected this guy would face rejection. But to my surprise, Mr. Nude was indeed a rice queen, as he welcomed the overtures. Mr. Asian started affectionately stroking Mr. Nude's cock. Then, in a squatting position, he began to blow on Mr. Nude. In a matter of seconds, they attracted a crowd, with a few men body worshipping Mr. Nude's toned physique.

Mr. Nude, not amused, quickly left, followed by Mr. Asian. I remained in the porn room to observe whether other individuals would engage in additional open sex activities. A bit later, I headed off to the darkroom, where I encountered Mr. Asian and Mr. Nude fucking. Mr. Nude was bending over while Mr. Asian was pounding his ass. Mr. Nude, a white guy, is a bottom? You shouldn't be surprised. It has always been my experience that rice queens are primarily bottoms. I believe Mr. Asian lacked experience with the topping process. His cock kept slipping out, and he had trouble getting it back in. What a waste, I thought. So many more experienced tops could have done wonders with that creamy white ass. I only watched them in action for a few minutes before I made my hasty exit.

Later, I encountered Mr. Nude in the locker area. He dressed, put on his sunglasses, and then left. I'm uncertain if he took a shower after his sexual encounter. But he got what he came for. To get fucked—mission accomplished. I guess he felt satisfied as he walked out of the dark bathhouse and into the afternoon sunshine.

.

Chapter 4
In Search Of A Third Mouth

When you enter the steam room at the baths, you often find sex already in progress. The other day I entered the steam room at 9 AM. Judging by the action, you would have thought it was midnight. Three couples were engaging in sexual intercourse in the steam room, and no one had yet consumed their morning coffee. They were screwing one guy, blowing off another, and passionately kissing a third.

Today, a fresh day in the sauna was no different. As usual, it was dark, and you could only see shadows. But the longer you stay in the dark, the more your eyes adjust. So eventually, you will see things much more clearly.

One guy was sitting on the top bench, back against the wall, enjoying a blowjob. The other guy positioned himself strategically, placing himself in front of the other guy to suck him off. The darkness obscured my vision, revealing only two bodies involved in intimate activities. I hung around the steam room to catch a glimpse of them. The person giving head was Mr. Younger, who had a great body. Mr. Older, who possessed an average physique, was the receiver. I was curious to see if this relationship was between a customer and a hustler. I have seen my share of couplings like this before. An hour later, I walked past them in the hallway and observed Mr. Younger guiding Mr. Older around, as this was Mr. Older's first visit to a bathhouse. Perhaps this wasn't a typical customer-hustler relationship. Maybe these two guys met on the Internet and hooked up at the baths.

Later I was sitting in the porn room, and who should walk in? Mr. Younger and Mr. Older. They sat almost right next to me as I got a bird's-eye view of this coupling. Soon, a small group of guys began to gather around them, eagerly stroking themselves off in anticipation of a potential sex show. They weren't disappointed. A new guy, Mr. Cute, walked in and noticed Mr. Younger. Eyes locked as Mr. Cute stepped forward to get closer. Mr. Younger said, "Suck me off, and my friend will suck you off. Deal?"

These three individuals formed a triangle as Mr. Cute was sucking off Mr. Younger, who was leaning against the wall. In turn, Mr. Older was sucking off Mr. Cute in a squatting position. The trio engaged in a marathon of slurping, sucking, moaning, and feeling each other up. Mr. Younger appeared unfazed, as if it were just another day at the office. He was neither really into it nor turned on by it. While it was hugely enjoyable, it didn't seem to be an earth-shattering event for him. Mr. Younger acted more like a director, saying, "Oh yeah, man, feel it. Suck that big cock off."

Just as it began, it abruptly came to an end. After expressing his gratitude to Mr. Younger, Mr. Cute departed in pursuit of fresh meat. The audience, which had gathered to watch, quickly dispersed to seek action elsewhere. That was the end of that, I thought.

Walking the halls later on, I noticed a crowd watching something. Curious, I peeked in and saw the duo of Mr. Younger and Mr. Older once again in action. This performance featured a new member, yet the arrangement remained unchanged.

The new individual was able to effectively suck Mr. Younger off by standing on a bench. This new person leaned forward in an attempt to swallow and suck as much of Mr. Younger's cock as possible. Mr. Older, in his usual squatting position, was happily sucking off the new guy.

It's fascinating to observe that Mr. Younger would only suck Mr. Older's cock. He declined to suck the cocks of the other two men. Mr. Younger seemed to be selective about who he would suck, which is a common practice at the baths. Get used to it.

Chapter 5
Chub & Chaser Sweat Fest

While strolling through the baths' hallways, I came across a man I had seen several times. He was a bespectacled Asian man, but I was uncertain about his specific ethnic background. Japanese, Chinese, Korean, or Filipino? I was unsure. Whenever I encountered him, he consistently sought a larger individual for sexual activity. Yes, you read that right—an Asian actively seeking a chubby individual for sex.

This contradicts the stereotype that every Asian man desires a muscular white man. This Asian had a strong preference for chubby white men; the chubbier, the better. Every third week, the bathhouse would host an event called "Chubs at the Tubs," and he would always be there dutifully. I had witnessed him constantly interacting and mingling with other obese, larger men. But I never saw him in action until now.

Walking into the steam room, I saw Mr. Asian sucking Mr. Chub's cock. Mr. Asian was sitting on the lower bench, face forward toward Mr. Chub, who was sitting on the higher bench. Mr. Asian was genuinely delighted to be sucking Mr. Chub's cock; he was even slurping Mr. Chub's balls. This was all to the delight and joy of Mr. Chub.

But that was not enough. Oh no, we have just begun. Mr. Chub got up, turned around, and leaned against the wall, legs spread. Mr. Asian bent his tall, limber legs into a squatting position. Then Mr. Asian buried his face into Mr. Chub's round ass and began to ferociously consume that delectable anal region. Mr. Asian really got into it, enthusiastically, sucking and tongue-fucking Mr. Chubs' tight hole. Mr. Asian would alternately focus on various areas of Mr. Chub's buttocks. He would work on the cheeks, fuck the hole, suck the balls, and caress Mr. Chub's cock. Throughout this suckfest, Mr. Asian maintained his cock's hard-rock erection.

The steam room was getting progressively hotter, and I'm not just talking about the physical heat. Mr. Chub seemed to want to take a breather to get some fresh air. But Mr. Asian was so totally into Mr. Chub that he wouldn't let him out of his clutches.

Mr. Asian lay down on the bench, face up. Showing off his smooth skin and long-limbed body, he motioned for Mr. Chub to squat under his mouth. Then the rimming continued and continued. There was tongue fucking, ball slurping, and cock sucking. It went on over and over again as Mr. Asian's cock remained incredibly rock-hard throughout.

Mr. Chub maintained his squatting position over Mr. Asian's face. However, he would periodically change his posture. He would turn around, his butt cheeks directed toward Mr. Asian, who would gleefully rim his hole. He would then pivot, positioning his cock directly above Mr. Asian's face, ready for it to be sucked off.

Eventually, dehydration forced Mr. Chub and Mr. Asian to leave the steam room. Both were dripping wet and needed oxygen. It was quite the sweatfest, and the steam had nothing to do with it!

Chapter 6
Older East Indian Dude Gets Lucky

Depending on your bathhouse, it may be common to witness staff members transforming into customers, now boogying down the baths' hallways. If you're not accustomed to seeing the bathhouse staff without any clothes, it can be jarring. Alternatively, it could be a fulfilling realization. The staff members you find attractive are suddenly revealing their true selves.

Bryce had worked at the baths for less than a year. We were friendly, and he seemed to be an upstanding guy. Coming from the suburbs, Bryce was new to the urban gay jungle. However, his loneliness would not last long, as he embodied the quintessential twink. He is a blonde Caucasian with zero body fat and a charming smile. I was impressed with his wisdom as he exuded a grounded and wise demeanor, despite his youth.

With his looks, he could have any fellow White Twink he wanted. However, Bryce chose a different path. He dates an East Indian guy who still lives with his parents. They are roughly the same age and have the same body type. They seemed perfect for each other and looked wonderful together. I have always believed that East Indian men, with their Caucasian features, hold a higher status than Asian men for sex.

I have spoken about racism in the past, so it was refreshing to see Bryce looking beyond the color of one's skin. The younger gay generation appears to be much more open-minded about looking past skin color and seeing the person. Or so I thought.

I was walking around when I spotted Bryce in the showers. His shift was over, and I guess he wanted to shower before going home. Or perhaps he simply wanted a quick fix of gay sex before he left for the day. It is not uncommon for the bathhouse staff to seek a quickie after their shift. I then saw him dart into the steam room. However, as soon as Bryce entered the steam room, he quickly stepped out again. However, I wanted to sit in the steam room, so I went inside and sat on one of the benches.

I was enjoying the steam when, all of a sudden, Bryce came back in. Since I was already sitting there, I didn't bother to leave. Although we are on friendly terms, I am aware that Bryce has no sexual interest in me. If my presence makes him uncomfortable, he is welcome to address it.

As Bryce kept entering and exiting the steam room, I observed an attractive man, approximately ten years older than Bryce, cruising him. He had showered beside Bryce, followed him around, and tried to give him the sign that he was available.

There we were, Bryce, Mr. Older, a few assorted guys, and me. All of us were sitting in the steam room, waiting to see what would happen. An Asian guy approached Bryce, which led Bryce to walk away and stand at the other end of the steam room. Bryce was sending the signal, "I'm not interested."

Then something did happen. But it was not what I had expected.

An older, and I mean older, East Indian man sat on the fringes, observing this cruising activity. Before

I knew it, Mr. Older East Indian and Bryce started feeling each other up.

Seated near me, Mr. Older East Indian turned towards Bryce and proceeded to suck him off. Whether it was out of modesty or embarrassment at my presence, Bryce used his towel to obstruct his cock, preventing anyone from witnessing him receive oral sex.

The men cruising Bryce made a hasty exit, realizing they had no chance with him. Eventually, it was just the three of us. I walked towards the far end of the steam room to give them some privacy. They, in turn, continued their sexual interlude at the other end. I couldn't determine what they were doing because of all the steam. What I could tell was that they were sitting side by side. It is probable that they were engaging in physical contact, kissing each other's wet bodies, and exchanging a messy embrace.

It appears that Bryce has a strong affinity for East Indian men, regardless of their age. That is truly refreshing.

Chapter 7
The Perfect Adonis

People use the porn room not only for watching porn, but also for socializing, cruising, and even for getting a blowjob. One day I was in the porn lounge, sitting off to the side, hidden by darkness, when he walked in. He was a gorgeous Adonis, 5'10, with a lean body, great long legs, a nice chest, and a pretty face. Unfortunately, beauty often comes with an attitude, and Mr. Adonis was no exception.

He sat on one of the bleachers, unwrapped his towel, and stretched his legs wide, letting it all hang out. He immediately started stroking his big, fat cock until it was fully erect. Mr. Adonis spent his time striking his fully erect dick against the sides of his legs while alternately stroking it. He was promoting his desire for a blowjob in public. But no one seemed interested in sucking him off dry.

There was no shortage of guys walking past him. Some men probably felt intimidated by Mr.

Adonis. Being around someone as beautiful as him, some feel he is outside their reach. That brings up an intriguing contradiction. Good-looking guys, some of whom may even be straight, prowl the halls looking for a blowjob. But looks always supersede technique. Some guys possess exceptional sucking skills. However, if their appearance is below average, they face rejection. Couldn't some of these hunks close their eyes and enjoy the sucking? This choosiness is to be expected. Whether you like it or not, a bathhouse is a superficial environment. Mr. Adonis wasn't interested in spending his time in the dimly lit area, hoping for an anonymous blowjob. Obviously, he was selective about who would suck his cock.

After maintaining and stroking his rock-hard erection for an extended period, someone finally approached Mr. Adonis. One slightly overweight man mustered the courage to make a move. Mr. Adonis's erection immediately went limp, and he crossed his legs to hide his cock. With that being the only nibble of interest, Mr. Adonis wrapped his towel around his waist and got up to leave.

That was the end of that, or so I thought. I was sitting in the steam room when Mr. Adonis entered. He followed the same pattern he used in the porn lounge. He sat on one of the bleachers, unwrapped his towel, and started stroking his big piece of meat. An Asian guy, who had followed him from the porn room to the steam room, approached him.

Mr. Asian used his hands to feel up Mr. Adonis's legs as foreplay to get him hard. Pretty soon, Mr. Asian swallowed Mr. Adonis's cock and started to suck it off hungrily. Was Mr. Adonis enjoying his blowjob? It was challenging to determine his enjoyment, as he exhibited no signs of emotion or sentiment. He simply sat there, absorbing everything with a blank expression. While Mr. Asian was enjoying his cock, Mr. Adonis remained stoic. His emotions were akin to receiving a pedicure while avoiding any physical contact with Mr. Asian. Eventually, Mr. Adonis pulled out a bottle of poppers and began snorting to get high. In between his snorts, Mr. Adonis used his hands every now and then to feel Mr. Asian's back. But that was it.

It lasted just 10 minutes. All the while, Mr. Adonis sat there, expressionless, taking it all in. Eventually, Mr. Adonis said he had to take a break and exited the steam room. After he cooled himself off with a shower, he hit the halls again, looking for someone to blow him.

Mr. Adonis wound up in the porn room doing the same thing. He stroked his cock and looked for someone to give him a blowjob. When I passed by, Mr. Adonis immediately threw his towel over his cock. Guess I'm not his type.

.

Chapter 8
Hungry To Suck

His name is Martin. He is 40ish, rough-looking, with tattoos and long hair tied into a ponytail. Did I mention he is married and straight? So, what's he doing at the baths? Well, he loves cock. Let me rephrase that. He absolutely loves cock. However, he considers himself very straight. He has no attraction toward men. However, he has an insatiable appetite for sucking cocks. When he spots a dick hanging out, he exclaims, "Wowza!"

Martin is in a quandary because he loves women but not men. But when he sees an erect penis, you better get out of the way. He enjoys slurping someone's dick for hours on end. However, he doesn't like other guys touching him when performing oral sex. Martin will not kiss or touch any guy while sucking. All he wants to do is suck cock.

Martin is from a suburban blue-collar area and shares access to a computer with his wife. Paranoid about his wife monitoring his search history, he doesn't dare pursue local hookups online. But he did hear about the baths, and that is where he goes to get his fix. Martin considers himself straight, and going into a gay environment intimidates and scares him. However, the temptation and desire for an erect cock are too strong for him to ignore. Every time he goes to the baths, he must down a couple of liquor shots to get comfortable.

When I first saw Martin at 10 a.m., he was walking around naked, except for wearing a hooded jacket. He had been at the baths since 4 a.m., engaging in cock sucking all night long. Martin told me if there's a cock with a pulse, he will suck it. His record for cock sucking was in college. He spent an entire day—8 hours with a few breaks—sucking off his coach's cock.

Martin's favorite way to suck is for the recipient to repeatedly say the word "fag" while he slurps away. Afterwards, he enjoys cum shooting all over his face or inside his mouth. However, the thought of another guy touching him while sucking repulses Martin.

Martin loves his wife, but he can't give up on Cock. To satisfy his needs, he has asked his wife to consider a three-way relationship involving two men and himself. Unfortunately for Martin, his wife has consistently rejected the idea. However, he revealed to me that he had previously been in a four-way relationship, which involved two men and two women. Martin said having an MTF (male to female) fuck buddy would fulfill his dreams. His objective is to locate an individual who bears a striking resemblance to a woman, including breasts, yet still possesses a penis. Since he shares a computer with his wife, how could he connect with those types of trans people without his wife finding out his search history online? The only solution he found was to visit gay baths.

Martin feels compelled to visit the gay baths to satisfy his sexual cravings for cock. As time passed, Martin's behavior became increasingly strange. I saw him on a Saturday afternoon one weekend, which wasn't unusual. However, Martin's excessive drinking led him to become less diligent in concealing his double life. Martin told his wife he was going camping for the weekend. But in reality, he was spending the weekend at the baths. Martin struggled to handle the situation. First, his wife forced him to take the dog on his trip! His wife asked, "How can you go camping and not take the dog with you?" Since the gay baths do not allow pets, Martin had no choice but to lock his dog in his car. However, he intended to check on his dog about every four hours. Martin likely didn't want to spend the money on a kennel. Next, he planned to use his debit card to pay his bathhouse fee. Then, he promptly turned off his cell phone and proceeded to chase down every cock in the building while also taking shots of liquor every 15 minutes.

After 24 hours, his wife was frantic, unable to reach him. She investigated his debit card transactions online and discovered an unusual charge in the city. She believed he was in the woods. Has someone stolen her husband's debit cards? Did someone kidnap him, putting him in danger? Unaware of the bathhouse concept, she proceeded to contact the listed location for the debit charges. She asked if her husband was there and what the place was like. The bathhouse staff refused to say if her husband was there. However, they did inform her what type of place a bathhouse was. Panicked, she filed a missing person report. Meanwhile, Martin became increasingly intoxicated as he engaged in oral sex with multiple partners.

I'm uncertain about the outcome of this scenario. All I know is that I still see Martin at the gay baths. No matter what story he told his wife, she must have bought it.

Chapter 9
Getting Lucky In The Sauna

Occasionally, it's impossible to predict when or where a sexual encounter will occur. Some guys can lie in a sling, with their legs up, and nothing happens. You are lying there for hours, waiting for someone to notice you. I recall encountering a man at the baths who was lying face down on his bed, eagerly anticipating sex. Nobody showed interest. He wasn't bad-looking and would have been a wonderful fuck for somebody. That's what happens if there are more bottoms than tops at the baths.

However, the perfect alignment of all the planets is necessary for a fantastic fuck to happen at the baths. The tubs are all about luck and timing; you can't plan for these events. It is important to be ready when the opportunity presents itself. One day I walked into the wet sauna and happened upon a fuck session already in progress. They discarded their towels while their wet, naked bodies engaged in intimate activities. Mr. Bottom was lying face up while Mr. Top was squatting. Mr. Bottom maneuvered his knees behind his ears so he could enjoy that cock inside of him.

For Mr. Top, the squatting position required a lot of stamina. The sauna's heat does not allow many people to continue in that vein for an extended period of time. Prompting them to change positions. Mr. Bottom got up and leaned up against the bench, face forward. Then he stuck his ass out like a sore thumb.

Mr. Top inserted his finger into his mouth to get it wet with saliva. He then fingered and loosened Mr. Bottom's hole as deeply and hard as possible. Mr. Bottom, who appeared to enjoy the intermission between the fucks, let out joyful wails. Mr. Top prepared himself for a secure and satisfying fuck by withdrawing his finger and spreading his legs. Then BANG, he started to fuck. He repeatedly pumped his firm cock into Mr. Bottom's ass.

Mr. Bottom was thoroughly enjoying the massage of his prostate as he screamed shrieks of pure ecstasy between Mr. Top's pumping grunts. Mr. Top maintained his position, aware of the extent to which Mr. Bottom was enjoying this fuck. As the powerful thrusts of his fucking continued, Mr. Top held firm to Mr. Bottom. He then started to kiss his back and neck tenderly, then nuzzled his ears while pinching his nipples. Mr. Top was tender and tough at the same time while continuing to pound without stopping.

Not long after, a crowd began to gather to observe this extraordinary fuck session in the sauna. One good-looking guy got up close. Mr. Good-Looking was practically standing next to them. He started stroking his cock while wearing a towel around his waist. Mr. Top desired something more, so he removed Mr. Good-Looking's towel between thrusts and began to stroke Mr. Good-Looking's cock.

As Mr. Top continued to fuck, Mr. Bottom wanted to get in on the action. While Mr. Top continued to fuck him, Mr. Bottom moved closer to Mr. Good-Looking and began to kiss him with hunger. This three-way fuck continued for a few minutes until Mr. Top started approaching the point of ejaculation.

As he began to inject his hot ejaculate into Mr. Bottom's loose anus, Mr. Top let out a heart-stopping scream. As all three exhaled, Mr. Good-Looking slapped the other two men on the back and expressed thanks. At this point, dehydration from prolonged exposure to the hot sauna necessitated water and oxygen for all three. While Mr. Good-Looking made a quick exit, Mr. Top withdrew his cock, and Mr. Bottom turned around to ensure Mr. Top was still wearing a condom. Mr. Top removed the condom that was on his dick and held it up for him to see. They kissed each other and hugged. Then they parted ways to shower off this latest sex encounter before hitting the halls to look for a new one.

Chapter 10
The Sounds Of Sex

Hearing the sounds of sex can be a significant turn-on, just like watching gay porn. As a frequent visitor to the baths, you will undoubtedly hear plenty of intimate activities taking place behind closed doors. Rows and rows of closet-sized rooms constrict the bathhouse's space. It is the same as a commercial airplane. Airlines aim to squeeze in as many seats as possible to make money. The baths have the same concept. More rooms mean more customers, thus more money. Naturally, many bathhouse patrons eavesdrop, whether they like it or not. Being in such close quarters, you overhear some of the most intimate encounters.

Not too long ago, a moderately hairy guy occupied the room next to me. He was lying face-up with a towel barely covering his midsection. Another guy, fully dressed in glasses, was walking around. It was summer, and he was dressed in a shirt, shorts, and sandals. Cruising up and down the hallways, he looked exasperated. He seemed to believe that he was squandering his time.

He then approached my neighbor, Mr. Hairy. I was in my room and could not tell what was happening next door. However, I could see Mr. Glasses in the hallway, staring into the room next to mine. He cruised outside Mr. Hairy's door, rubbing his hands over his shorts. Mr. Hairy must have liked what he saw because the door suddenly closed.

I could not see what was going on, but I could hear. Slurping accompanied a creaking sound, which I assumed was the mattress. This encounter went on for a few minutes. Then the sound stopped, and I heard more creaking noises. I could hear the ripping sound of Velcro as I assumed Mr. Glasses was removing his sandals and kicking them off. The sound of keys jangled as he simultaneously took off his shorts and underwear. Subsequently, the sound of a t-shirt pulling up over Mr. Glasses' head resonated. Yes, he was naked, and I could hear the gentle sound of plastic falling onto the nightstand. Obviously, he had taken off his glasses.

I next heard Mr. Glasses get on top of Mr. Hairy. The sounds of kissing, lip-smacking, and heavy breathing followed. After a while, I started to hear more slurping, which probably meant someone was receiving oral, and the other guy was giving. Someone was sighing heavily and saying, "Oh God," repeatedly. Amidst all this, I caught the sound of someone inhaling poppers. Then, I heard someone performing a handjob. The sound was similar to the rubbing of wet plastic back and forth. I suspect someone was using lube or their pre-cum as a lubricant for this particular jack-off.

I continued to listen to the noise of slurping, kissing, sucking, and sniffing. The sounds of bodies shifting positions and the creaking of the mattress persisted for some time. Eventually, non-stop slurping noises went on, with one guy exclaiming "Fuck" and "Oh God" repeatedly. I suspect that someone was rimming, preparing for the main event.

The mattress continued to creak as these guys moved into their positions. The sound of tearing open a condom pierced the air. Then there was a moment of silence, followed by a loud yelp. The mattress resumed its creaking noise. As time went on, the creaking of the mattress not only got louder but also faster as well. In between the creaking of the mattress was the sound of one guy going, "AHHH, AHHH, AHHH!" He repeated "AHHH, AHHH, AHHH!" after each pounding, he received.

Meanwhile, the person on top was emitting grunts and intensifying his thrusts deeper and deeper. Judging by the creaking sound at certain intervals, positions were changing. They may have performed a flip-fuck, which involves the bottom and top positions changing. Nonetheless, this act was not some five-minute anal session. The process continued for a considerable amount of time, with the mattress resuming its consistent creaking. The sounds of moving bodies followed, and then the mattress began to creak again.

The two men started to settle into their roles. The bed's movement against the wall, the mattress's creak, the head's impact on the headboard, and the ecstatic shouts from both men filled my ears. Indeed, we are nearing the end.

One guy exclaims, "Oh, fuck, yeah, give it to me; ride me, oh fuck." The other guy kept repeating,

"AHHH, AHHH, AHHH!" They screamed those words as if they were torture. Then came the panting sound of "AHHH, AHHH, AHHH!" as if someone was experiencing an asthma attack. The words "Fuck, fuck, fuck" and "I'm going to cum" followed the shriek. The other guy yells out, "Yeah, baby." Then both men simultaneously let out a spine-tingling scream. I guess they both came together at the same time.

Then there was nothing but silence. The two probably collapsed on top of each other, obviously exhausted from their sex workout session.
Then one of the guys asked the other one this fundamental question. "So, what's your name?"

Chapter 11
Body Worshipped At The Baths

Unlike anal and oral, body worship is not something you see openly done at the baths. But it doesn't mean that it never happens. Meet Mr. Body, a 6-foot-tall hunk with a fabulously toned physique. You'd think he would have trouble finding that type of action at the baths. But he doesn't.

Those with a physique akin to a meticulously sculpted clay statue typically receive invitations to participate in body worship sessions. That doesn't describe Mr. Body. Although his body is impressive, it is not inherently rock-hard and muscular. So instead of trolling the online body-worshiping posts on hook-up sites, Mr. Body heads straight to the baths. He takes off his clothes, revealing only a tiny bathing suit. He lowers his trunks to reveal his latissimus dorsi muscle (lats). Then he makes his way to the darkroom located on the top floor.

The darkroom is just that: complete pitch darkness. You must feel your way through the room while faceless sex occurs. No one can see you, and you cannot see anyone else. You have no idea who is there and can only assess the person based on your touch and feel. It is the epitome of anonymous sex. There are drawbacks, because, let's face it, most gay men are superficial. Personally, I want to see the person's face. The guys you find hanging out in the darkroom typically consist of visible minorities, overweight individuals, and elderly gay men. These men are at the bottom of gay society, so any action is better than none. That's why these men are gathering in the darkroom.

These types of guys don't matter to Mr. Body. Regardless of who is pawing and fawning, he craves body worship. His M.O. is always the same. Mr. Body walks into the darkroom, leans against a wall, and waits. He doesn't have to wait long before four to five pairs of hands begin attacking his body. They pull down his small bathing suit, grope him, jack him off, feel him up, pin him, massage his butt, and so on. The jacking off rapidly escalates into a series of blowjobs, with some of the men alternately sucking his cock. Simultaneously, two different guys will start sucking each of Mr. Body's nipples. In pure bliss, Mr. Body takes it all in. However, whenever someone attempts to kiss him, he would turn his head away, as kissing is just too intimate for some guys. Mr. Body's refusal to move from his standing position also frustrated some guys as they attempted to remove his bathing suit completely. But Mr. Body kept his feet firmly on the floor, his trunks resting on the ground between his legs. He took all precautions to prevent his body worshipers from stealing his bathing suit.

Mr. Body soon grew weary of this fawning group and left. To clarify, the fawning did not exhaust him. He just wanted a different group of admirers. Therefore, he relocated to a different section of the darkroom, remained motionless, and patiently awaited the resumption of this worship session to start all over again. Mr. Body would reenact this scenario repeatedly for hours, with men from various sections of the darkroom worshiping his body.

It can be challenging to distinguish between different individuals in the darkness. This is what makes Mr. Body unique: his lack of prerequisites.

He disregards factors such as an individual's age, weight, race (Black or Asian), autism, or wheelchair confinement. When hands and mouths worship his body, he is in pure bliss.

At the baths, Mr. Body seeks action in both darkness and light. One day, he ventured into the porn area, as there appeared to be minimal activity in the darkroom. He donned a towel instead of his skimpy Speedo. Mr. Body lay on his back and positioned himself to flaunt his crotch. It didn't take long for someone to pick up the signal. One homely and much older Asian guy began sweeping his hand over Mr. Body's chest. Soon, Mr. Asian discarded the towels and began lying down on Mr. Body. Some guys passed by and started feeling up Mr. Body, even asking if he wanted to go to their private room. Mr. Body declined, and soon it was just the two of them, with Mr. Asian giving Mr. Body a blowjob. Positions changed as Mr. Body stood up, with both arms stretched out, holding on to the partition walls. Mr. Asian was squatting, sucking off Mr. Body's big cock. Mr. Body was pumping his dick in and out of Mr. Asian's mouth, causing his butt to gyrate in response. However,

Mr. Body wasn't looking at Mr. Asian or reciprocating affection. Instead, he turned his head to the TV monitor showing the porn. The hotter the porn got, the faster his thrusts increased. Therefore, Mr. Body was exploiting Mr. Asian as a real-life sexual object. Hopefully, Mr. Asian got something out of it.

This blowjob lasted for 30 minutes, as Mr. Asian showed no signs of slowing down. How many opportunities like this would Mr. Asian get? Such opportunities are rare, so Mr. Asian seized them completely. Pretty soon, Mr. Body got bored. He withdrew, thanked Mr. Asian, and then proceeded to search for other individuals to adore his body. Final footnote. It's peculiar that Mr. Body appears to engage in this devotion solely on weekends and during the daytime. He comes in at 9 AM and leaves 8 hours later. Could he be concealing his involvement in this bathhouse activity from a significant other? Could it be someone of a different gender? Could he be bi? I recently saw him exit the baths one day. Once on the street, he held his head low so no one would see him. Who is he hiding this bathhouse secret from? I'm sure we would all love to know.

.

Chapter 12
Some Guys Have All The Luck

Guys often arrive at the baths with a sense of arrogance and entitlement. They exude an air of superiority, as if they are a gift from God. They are so attractive that they don't consider anyone else unless they meet their elevated standards. The irony is that some of these men are not even that outstanding-looking. However, they still believe they can attract attention, leading them to behave like jerks around other men.

We have all seen guys acting like this. This behavior is prevalent everywhere, including the gym, clubs, and bars. These characteristics are particularly noticeable at the baths, and understandably so. These guys know they are hot (or think so). They are aware that as soon as they step into the baths, other men will inevitably gravitate toward them.

One day, I came across a man who perfectly embodied this attitude. He was around 40, with a shaved head and a slender, fit body. I wouldn't say he was a hunk, but he wasn't ugly, either. He was above average in the looks department, but his physical attractiveness was not exceptional. However, he did have an arrogance that gave off the vibe that he was better than everyone.

He walked into the steam room and surveyed the crowd. There he spotted a young blond twink who was stunning. He was indeed a beauty with an exceptionally sculpted body. Mr. Arrogance made a beeline toward Mr. Twink, thinking he would score.

The steam room has a set of bleachers where customers can sit. There are top and bottom benches (how fitting!). Mr. Twink was sitting on the top bench, so Mr. Arrogance slithered near him, positioning himself on the bottom bench.

Mr. Twink had his eyes closed. His body was ramrod stiff, which I found strange. Here is somebody, not bad looking, moving towards him. You'd think Mr. Twink wouldn't be that repulsed or turned off. But that is how he was acting. The vibe

Mr. Twink gave was, "Stay away from me; I'm not interested."

But that wasn't stopping Mr. Arrogance. Despite Mr. Twink's shut eyes and his body stiffening, Mr. Arrogance was inching closer and closer. With his gaze fixed on Mr. Twink, Mr. Arrogance placed his hand on his leg. Mr. Twink did not respond. Undeterred, Mr. Arrogance began feeling up Mr. Twink, sensually moving his hand back and forth on Mr. Twink's leg.

Then a big 400-pound bear walked into the steam room. Mr. Bear looked like a teddy bear but much older and quite humongous. He spotted this sex act in the making and moved closer to take a look. Before you could say anything, Mr. Bear and Mr. Twink began to kiss passionately. Mr. Twink's cock immediately swelled, protruded, and hardened. Mr. Arrogance interpreted the sensation as a signal and began to jack off Mr. Twink's erect cock. But soon, it became evident that Mr. Twink was into bears, which is why he didn't respond to Mr. Arrogance's overtures. Did I mention that it was also Bear Day at the baths that particular afternoon?

Soon, Mr. Twink and Mr. Bear were settling into a rhythm. In between the kissing, they were pawing each other hungrily. Mr. Arrogance soon realized that he was the odd man out in this scenario and let go of Mr. Twink's cock. He was likely accustomed to being the center of attention. In the past, men outside his league would watch and want to join Mr. Arrogance's antics. However, Mr. Arrogance now finds himself observing from an outside perspective. Therefore, Mr. Arrogance walked away, acknowledging his defeat, in search of someone else who could appreciate his body.

Mr. Bear was sucking off Mr. Twink's huge, powerful cock as he genuinely enjoyed it. Letting them have some privacy, I left. But later on, I encountered them in the whirlpool as Mr. Bear was holding Mr. Twink. Eavesdropping on their conversation, I heard Mr. Twink complain about how hard it is to find a good bear. He used to go to another bathhouse that primarily catered to twinks. But he could never find a bear. Staff and management often wondered if he was a virgin or recently came out. Mr. Twink was handsome. Yet, he never seemed to get any action and always left the baths empty-handed. He did not utilize his time at the baths effectively. But today, Mr. Twink said, was time well spent.

.

Chapter 13
Look Alike Duo Having Fun

The other day in the grocery store, I noticed two bespectacled guys holding hands in one of the food aisles. There's nothing unusual about that, but in this instance, the pair could be mistaken for twins. They were the same height and hair color, seemed the same age, and even dressed in the same manner. However, they were two distinct individuals who shared a striking similarity in appearance.

The point of this story is to show how guys tend to want to date or fuck guys who are similar to them. They want a partner who is the same race and age, has a similar height, and possesses common interests. In the gay community, opposites don't attract.

I bring this phenomenon up because nowhere is it more prevalent than at the baths. If you are cruising the halls and see somebody you find cute, ask yourself this. Are you on the same level as he is? Are you comparable to the couple I previously discussed? Are you the same height, body type, age, and race? If not, it may not be worth your time.

Now, let's get to the main point of this story. It was a relaxed summer afternoon when this duo hit the outdoor patio at the baths. They looked like twins: brunette, tall, lean, and well-defined. They could pass as brothers. Instead of lounging around in their towels, they were shirtless, wore jeans, and enjoyed the sun. I suspected they had met for the first time at the baths and had just spent the past 12 hours together. They had enjoyed each other's company, drinking and snorting party drugs. The wearing of the jeans was their half-baked attempt to leave, but something was holding them back. Namely, the drugs were still making them horny, and they wanted to fool around some more.

There they stood, both clad in cozy jeans and brimming with passion. This dynamic duo decided to make out among the other men tanning around them. They began kissing while unzipping each other's jeans. Brunette #1 pulls down Brunette #2's jeans halfway and starts sucking him off. Brunette

#2 is enjoying this blowjob while taking puffs of his cigarette. Other guys noticed, but this look-alike duo was only interested in men on their level. Yes, it is superficial, but isn't everyone? This phenomenon explains why group sex activities can have varying outcomes. An orgy can only function effectively if there is mutual attraction among all participants. If you have four or eight guys, everyone needs to feel attracted to each other. If a single member fails to elicit attraction, the entire group disintegrates. This situation is ironic because the main purpose of an orgy is to engage in unrestrained passion without hesitation. To fuck and suck wildly without any thought or pretense of what the other guys look like. But that doesn't happen because we gay men are superficial in situations like that.

Let's return to our duo dressed in jeans. One is indulging in sexual activity, while the other is relishing the opportunity to show off to other men. Their audience of other guys was eyeing them hungrily, wanting to join in. If two guys are having sex and someone else wants to join, they must be on their level. If not, they will face rejection. But with this duo still high on drugs, they didn't care what the other person looked like. They just wanted someone who could perform adequately. One older Black guy immediately went up to the two and began stroking one of the guys' cocks. Then this homely Asian guy came upon the trio and began sucking on the person's nipples while feeling his chest. These two guys were quite timid, not wanting to suck or fuck. Brunette #1 was not willing to tolerate any hesitation when it came to sex. He flung Brunette #2 face down on a chair, pulled off his pants, and started to fuck him. The Black and Asian guy just massaged Brunette #1's chest while he was pumping away. It went on for a few minutes before this brunette duo decided to stop and walk away. They left the Asian and Black guy standing there, wondering what to do next.

Putting their jeans back on, this brunette duo headed to the bar area and ordered two beers. But they still continued having sex. Brunette #2 rolled down Brunette #1's jeans and squatted in front of him. He then proceeded to start sucking his piece of meat. All the while, Brunette #1 was drinking his beer. In between the sucking, Brunette #2 would stand up and begin kissing Brunette #1. Brunette #2 would then kneel once more to resume the sucking.

Wanting to do something other than sucking, Brunette #1 turned Brunette #2 over and began spanking his ass. By this time, he had discarded his jeans entirely and put a towel around his waist. Once the spanking stopped, Brunette #2, wanting to repay the favor, leaned into Brunette #1. He then proceeds to suck him off yet again. Brunette #1 leans back, enjoying the blowjob and a few sips of beer. Soon, the two brunettes became bored and put their jeans back on. Then they walked hand in hand to look for more action in the hallways of the baths.

Chapter 14
Bathhouse Etiquette

First and foremost, bathhouses are places for men to have sex. It serves as a sexual playground where men can indulge in their desires and engage in sexual activities around the clock, akin to a 24-hour convenience store. Come to think of it, the baths are like a supermarket. You can shop for whatever you are looking for. In a bathhouse, you can choose from Latinos to Twinks, Bears to Chubs, Asians to Blacks—whatever type of guy you are interested in, you will find. Far more than bars or clubs, the baths have something for everyone.

There are two misconceptions about bathhouses. First, only dirty older men go to the baths. Second, only gorgeous men can get lucky at a bathhouse. Neither is true. As I mentioned at the start, there is something for everyone. Sometimes, men use the baths to find a specific "type" of guy they can't find anywhere else, such as an Asian, Chub, Bear, and so on.

Bathhouses can be found in various locations, ranging from a side street to an obscure neighborhood. Most times, there is no sign on the door. You walk in and see a cashier located behind a protective window. The wall will display the list of prices for purchasing a room or a locker. Renting a room will give you privacy. If you choose to rent a locker, which is less expensive than a room, you won't have any privacy, especially if you happen to meet someone attractive. Most bathhouses will allow you to lock up your valuables in a safe—like a watch, wallet, or jewelry. Once you pay, the cashier will buzz you in, and you can open the door. The door will automatically close behind you. There is no chance of any strangers walking in by accident.

Depending on where you live, you might be required to purchase a bathhouse membership. The reason? According to some state laws, a bathhouse can only operate as a private men's club. Therefore, each patron must possess a membership. Some bathhouses may only need you to fill out some information on a card. Other bathhouses, however, may request a photo ID. Whether you are in the closet or openly out, you needn't worry about your personal information being leaked.

To be profitable, bathhouses need customers. How would they be able to keep customers if they leak personal information? Not to worry, as bathhouses are very discreet when it comes to maintaining membership confidentiality. Therefore, you need not fear exposure. The upside is that memberships may also offer discounts if the customer plans on making multiple visits to the baths. After years of going to my regular bathhouse, I have recently purchased a membership. Since I go so often, it allows me to save money. Every bathhouse does not require a membership purchase. However, if your local bathhouse requires you to buy one, be prepared.

After arriving, undress, wrap the towel around your waist, and cruise. It would be best if you showered before you explored the hallways. That way, you are fresh for whoever you next encounter. Then, after you have done the deed, take another shower. This way, you can refresh yourself for the next guy you find. For some, taking three to five showers is not uncommon! That's how many times some guys get lucky at the baths. Some men are paranoid about foot fungus and bring slippers or sandals to protect their feet.

The baths consist of dozens of rooms, all lined up among a maze of hallways. You spend most of your time walking the halls looking for a score. Everyone knows why the other person is there. Guys lie in their rooms, observing other men as they pass by. Or they stand in the hallways, observing those who walk around them. Everybody is cruising everyone. There is even a bulletin board for people to advertise themselves. For example, the board displays the message, "Room 218, submissive bottom, shoot your load inside me." There are dozens of similar messages on the board.

All bathhouses will have a sauna, steam room, and multiple showers to clean up. Many will have a hot tub or a swimming pool, with some places having both. To pass the time, most have porno rooms. Condoms are free of charge, but you will have to pay for lube. Every bathhouse has a snack bar and a payphone. There is also a lounge area where you can sit and watch television. You can also enjoy reading gay magazines like Advocate and Instinct.

The rules are straightforward at the baths. You will know right away if someone likes you. They will make eye contact with you. If he initiates eye contact and you reciprocate, you can predict the outcome. Some guys will not make eye contact or even look away. You cannot take it personally. That is the most important bathhouse rule, but many find it challenging to understand.

What if an individual initiate's eye contact with you, and you are interested? Try stroking your dick or playing with your nipples. Touching can also be a helpful cruising tool. If you are sitting near someone, you may want to try playing footsies or reaching over and pinching his nipple. If you pass someone in the hallway, you may decide to have your hand brushed against him. Some older men will even be bold enough to grab a guy's crotch! You can do this light touching to gauge someone's interest. But don't throw yourself at him. That makes you look desperate, which is a turn-off for most men. If the guy turns and pushes you aside, walk away. Do not prolong the agony of trying to create something that will not happen. He is not interested.

If someone approaches you, that is not up to your standards; be gentle in turning him down. Remember the treatment you would expect. We have all been the recipients of rejection at one time or another. I usually tell guys that I am just walking around to get a feel for the place. If you want to be direct, say, "I am not interested." Do not say, "Get out of my face." That is rude, although you will come across guys who are that blunt.

Conversely, if someone turns you down, move on gracefully. Do not stalk the person and hang around outside his room. It makes him uncomfortable and makes you look like a fool. By obsessing over someone who is not interested, you might miss out on someone who is interested in you. That's why you move on when someone says, "No thanks."

When you begin exploring the rooms, you will find men lying on their beds in various positions. Lying face down means he wants anal. Sitting up could indicate a variety of intentions, but most likely it's just enjoyment. Kneeling on the floor, he says he wants oral. If you pass by a room and the guy looks away, it indicates a lack of interest. However, if he looks at you and starts stroking himself, you know where that will lead.

If you see two guys getting it on, wait for a signal that you can join in. A wink, nod, or even a hand wave is a signal. If there are no indications, they are not interested in a third party. They will gently or forcefully push you away if you try to join in. That is embarrassing, so wait for the signs.

Remember, this is a bathhouse where rejection happens every second. Therefore, you cannot take it personally; that is how it is. If you cannot accept that, the baths are not for you. If you leave with anything after reading these essays, leave with this. A bathhouse is a place where quickie sex is the norm. If you are looking for a long bonding experience with someone, you will not find that at a bathhouse. I am not saying that it cannot happen, but it is rare. Most times, at the baths, a man's focus is to get off and move on. It is the norm in a bathhouse environment for a guy to get up and leave—all within 30 seconds of reaching ejaculation.

Often, there is no exchange of pleasantries before or after sex. It wastes time because both of you are there—FOR THE SEX! So why spend time talking? Time and time again, a guy will get up, put his towel back on, and leave your room once the sex finishes, all without saying a word. Afterward, you may run into him roaming the hallways, looking for his next encounter. Some guys are insensitive enough to act like they've never seen you before. Again, you cannot take it personally. Gay bathhouses aim to facilitate effortless and speedy sexual encounters. You are not there to make friends. Some guys don't even stick around looking for round two. Satisfied by getting off, some immediately leave the baths. It is not rare for men to spend only 20 minutes on the premises. Why stay if they've achieved their goal of getting laid? But some guys in the closet feel guilty after having quickie sex. They find it cheap and sordid. These men run out of the baths guilt-ridden, vowing never to return. But that only lasts a few hours, and they return to the baths the next day.

I frequently receive the question, "Can you go to the baths as only an observer? Can you observe without attracting attention?" The answer is yes, and here is how you do it. Avoid undressing. No rule says you have to strip off all of your clothes. Being fully dressed is a sign to other men that you are off-limits. When customers see someone fully dressed, they assume that the person works at the baths. All patrons know the bathhouse staff is off-limits. My friend Ari will do just that. When he goes to the baths, he stays fully clothed, sits in a well-lit part of the bathhouse, and watches people pass by. No one bothers him. If Ari sees someone attractive, he will pursue his object of desire while fully clothed.

Above all, ensure your safety by using condoms and lube. Someone told me something that has stayed with me, which I will pass on to you. Do not do anything that you do not want to do. It is not worth it. Often, you will experience intense feelings of passion. Avoid feeling compelled to participate in risky sexual activities or anything that causes you discomfort, even for a brief moment. Around the corner, another guy will do what you want to do. So be patient.

I would like to offer my final advice on the Gay Baths.

Have Fun!

Chapter 15
The Politics of Gay Oral Sex

Oral sex is the most common sex act at the baths; you can see it everywhere. There is a significant amount of oral sex taking place in the whirlpool, shower area, and lounge. It is so commonplace that it seems to be a prerequisite to be a gay man—that you must participate in oral sex.

When people think of oral sex, most envision this personal, intimate bonding experience between two people who genuinely care for each other. You have the opportunity to fully give yourself to another person. However, gay men need to break free from the heterosexual mindset. Oral sex is not sacred in the gay community. Kissing is the equivalent of displaying intimate contact between two men. You can get a blow job anywhere. Guys want to save real, physical, and close contact, such as kissing, for a future boyfriend. Many men have told me they do not even kiss guys they may encounter at the baths. Oral sex? No problem. Anal? Pass the lube. But kissing? NO WAY! You would expect the situation to be reversed.

For instance, I've seen this one Caucasian guy at the baths for the past few years. I've spoken to him several times; he is gay, amiable, and cute! However, the sole activity he enjoys at the baths is performing blowjobs, and he has no other interests. He avoids kissing, hugging, and anal contact. He focuses solely on delivering oral sex to one individual after another. I think his record is fifty blowjobs in one night. He doesn't discriminate between races, ages, or the person's weight. I've seen him go from Black to White, fat to thin, old to young—just a variety of men. He only cares about the cock's size. I guess that's one reason I've never seen him suck an Asian cock.

On a regular basis, I've seen this other young, white guy at the baths. My opinion is that he identifies as straight but suppresses his desire for men. Whenever these cravings become overwhelming, he drops by the baths. I've seen him multiple times, at all hours of the day. All he does is give blowjobs every chance he gets. Once, I watched him become so engrossed in the act of sucking cock that he would slurp it as if it were his last meal, refusing to stop. The man receiving the blowjob appeared to feel ensnared, with no alternative but to remain seated, persist in watching the pornographic film, and relish the sensation.

Gay men aren't the only ones who enjoy getting their cock sucked off. You can find many straight guys prowling the gay baths seeking a blowjob. They have wives, girlfriends, or even fiancées who don't like to perform oral sex on their significant other. Many women find it gross. What should a man do if he is not getting it at home? They go to the baths. Many straight men don't consider oral sex adultery or even sex. They see it as a way to get off. Here's a method for identifying a straight man in the gay baths who wants a blow job: The man would be fully clothed, the zipper undone, with his cock hanging out. It gives a new meaning to the phrase "Well Hung!"

I remember one guy whose sole purpose for going to the gay baths was to get oral sex. Every week, he consistently showed up at the baths on the same day and time. He would situate himself in the porn room and start stroking himself. Then a succession of over twenty guys would suck him for over three hours! During that time, he would never say anything. Some blowjobs lasted a minute; others could go on longer. After three hours, he would shower, get dressed, and leave. Men waited for him in the porn room because of his popularity and consistency. At least 70% of those guys were Asian!

There are also places known as "glory holes." Men insert their penis through an opening, then wait for a passerby to suck them off. On one side, the person receiving doesn't know who is doing the sucking. The person on the other side is unaware of whose cock it is. All the guy sees is a cock hanging out of a hole, so he goes for it. This is a place where sex is truly anonymous! There is even a "slurp ramp"! That's where men stand next to each other, all in a row, sticking their dicks through a hole. On the other side, men can suck off the cocks one after the other.

Therefore, if you're a guy who loves to give, there's no shortage of cocks to suck. However, based on what I have seen at the baths, guys are more inclined to receive than to give. You'll notice that every example I write about involves guys who prefer to receive rather than give. Oral sex, in my opinion, primarily revolves around a power dynamic (a cock staring you in the face). Instead of allowing things to unfold naturally, the other person dictates the course of action. Many gay Asians, often perceived as passive participants, are particularly susceptible to this phenomenon.

After decades of going to the baths, I still see gay Asian men giving heads to anyone and everyone in record numbers. It is a never-ending cycle. I seldom observe a gay Asian man at the baths decline to engage in oral sex with an individual, no matter the age, even 70. It's no surprise that many older gay men find Asians attractive! However, in reality, it is a self-esteem issue, as many gay Asian men lack self-confidence. As a result, gay Asians seek validation from gay white men, who are considered the standard in the gay community. Therefore, in order to validate themselves, one must engage with as many gay white men as possible. But I also genuinely believe many white guys at the baths view Asians as the ultimate "backup." During their stay at the baths, they hunt for good-looking prey. However, if they are unsuccessful in finding anyone, they turn their attention to the desperate Asian man who is waiting in the wings.

It disturbs me that gay men only see us Asians as a way to serve them, like some concubines freely giving out blowjobs. After receiving oral pleasure from an Asian, these gay white men depart. They do not express gratitude, acknowledgment, or even a nod. Once they are satisfied, these gay white men wrap their towel around their midsection and depart to seek out other men. Those Asians would be on their knees, still in position, with their mouths open, getting nothing. Unless the Asian in question genuinely enjoys giving blowjobs, the only satisfaction these Asian men experience is a fleeting sense of fulfillment when they blow a White man. But it is a vicious cycle for these Asians. After blowing a Caucasian man, many of them feel used. However, five minutes later, they are already looking for another white man to blow. They do this in order to continue receiving the validation they desire.

Despite the risks of HPV (oral cancer) and other STIs associated with oral sucking, no one is using a condom. Gay guys won't suck cock while wearing a condom. That will not happen. What if you're one of the rare guys who uses condoms for oral sex? It depends on the person and how things are progressing. You can say immediately, "I do not engage in oral sex without a condom." Most of the time, you will have guys who become incredulous and leave without saying a word.

Surprisingly, you might find the odd guy who will put the condom on. If he likes you, he'll do anything you ask. However, this is a rare occurrence. However, there are some instances where a man expresses no interest in oral sex, and other circumstances arise. Alternatively, he engages in giving oral sex without seeking reciprocation. Of course, there are instances where things escalate quickly without any established ground rules. Suddenly, you find yourself staring at an erect penis right in your face. That is when you would say, "I just brushed my teeth" or "I just came from the dentist." If the guy leaves, he leaves. If you take anything away from this essay, make sure it's this one. Vaccinate against HPV to lower your risk of developing oral cancer. Speak with your family doctor about the vaccination process.

While I have just written about the politics and etiquette around oral sex, there is one topic I have not covered. I have not addressed the topic of ejaculating into a man's mouth. It would be best to always ask BEFOREHAND. It is unacceptable to squirt into a guy's mouth without asking. Most guys consistently inquire whether they can ejaculate in the mouth or not. At the very least, they would give a warning, indicating that they were close. Cumming in someone's mouth without asking or warning is just unacceptable manners.

So, after writing about the politics of oral sex, I hope I've clarified things for anyone new to the ins and outs of blowjobs. Just because every gay man performs oral sex doesn't mean you should. It isn't for everyone. Don't feel pressured to do it for one minute. Remember what I always say: Don't do anything you are uncomfortable doing.

Only you know what's best for you and no one else.

Chapter 16
Sex With Clothes On

While many gay men love gay baths, there are just as many men who are scared of the tubs. Those who have never been to a bathhouse are unsure about what lies on the other side, as it can be intimidating to venture into the unknown. The most frequent question I receive is:

Can I go to the baths as a voyeur? Can I visit the baths as an observer without fear of being cruised?

The answer is yes, and here is how to do it. Remain fully clothed.

No rule exists at the baths that says you must undress when you visit. Some men prefer to complement their towel look with a few items, such as a T-shirt. But a tiny minority of men want to remain fully clothed. By staying dressed, they are sending a strong signal to other guys that they are off-limits, so hands-off. The fully dressed customer is either a hustler, a bathhouse employee, or an observer, so other bathhouse patrons are unsure. I have always felt that when a guy keeps his clothes on, it is an issue of control. He wants to control whatever sexual situation he might find himself in. His clothes act as a barrier, almost like a shield, between himself and his sexual partner. If a sexual act happens while one is fully dressed, both men cannot get too close, as keeping clothes on makes the sexual liaison clinical and detached.

Keep this in mind, though. If you decide to stay clothed during your visits to the baths, you will have to be the aggressor if you want any action. Being naked puts you on equal footing with everyone else. Being fully dressed sends the signal to everyone that you are unapproachable.

I recall encountering a GORGEOUS and MUSCULAR blond man who resembled a porn star. He kept his jeans on, but he was shirtless and wore sunglasses. It was summer, and during that time, the baths felt more like a pool house. Men would enter and exit the outdoor patio. They would be completely naked or be wearing a towel, having spent their time swimming or tanning (yes, the bathhouse I go to does allow nude tanning and swimming!). The blond guy stood in the hallway for an hour without getting any action. Finally, he approached me, recognizing my approachable face, and asked me what was wrong with all these guys. Excuse me, I said. He told me he was from out of town, and he dropped in to check out the bathhouse situation in my city. He couldn't understand what was wrong with all of the local guys. Why wasn't anyone approaching him? I explained that because he was wearing sunglasses, no one could make eye contact to see where his interest lay. Wearing jeans, he conveys a non-approachable demeanor and is likely only seeking a blow job. Given his attractive appearance and impressive physique, many men mistakenly believe he is beyond their reach. "I am unapproachable" was the signal he was projecting. He thought briefly about what I said and then replied, "Nah, it must be the guys here." With that, he left to go to another bathhouse. However, his demeanor conveyed the message, "I should not engage in conversation until I approach you."

You must be scratching your head, wondering how men have sex when one is fully clothed. The guy who remains dressed is in total control of the situation. In short, he is selfish. He is using the other person as a plaything for his sexual gratification. Having one person fully dressed makes it difficult for anyone else to approach. That's the whole point. It's about avoiding intimacy for the person who keeps his clothes on. It is not like you are both taking turns pleasing each other. The guy in clothing is getting everything he desires.

But there are other reasons why some guys stay fully dressed at the baths. Other than the control issue, many guys do not want to give themselves totally to a stranger. Men use clothing as a protective barrier to distance themselves from sexual encounters. As previously mentioned, many guys want to save intimacy for a future boyfriend. Remember, we are not dealing with the heterosexual world here. We are interacting in the homosexual world, where the norms are completely different. In the gay world, you can get a blowjob or fuck anywhere. Many gay men want to save real intimacy, like kissing, for someone they love. Therefore, they refrain from any lip-locking at the baths.

For example, there are many high-powered men in finance who stop by the baths just to get a blowjob. There is no intimacy, no name exchange, and no connecting. All these businessmen want is a blowjob. They do not care who provides it, and most of these businessmen are straight! Where else can these men get a blowjob if their fiancée or wife finds oral sex repulsive? Bingo! They head to the baths. Going to the tubs in search of a blowjob is more cost-effective and discreet than hiring a hooker to perform the task. A hooker costs $60, whereas the special lunch rate at the baths is only 12 bucks. The cost of a five-minute blowjob is $2.50 per minute. These guys in finance know a bargain when they see it.

These straight businessmen stay dressed in their Armani suits and walk the hallways looking for a blowjob. The only difference is that their cocks hang out of an open fly. The message is clear—suck my cock. They walk up and down the halls until someone blows them off. Some even carry poppers so they can enjoy the blow job that much more. After ejaculation, these businessmen pee (to avoid any STIs), zip up their pants, and head out the door. No fuss, no muss, no cleanup. You're in and out of the baths in 15 minutes, completely satisfied.

On the other hand, you have fully dressed men who want to give, not receive. These guys are able to prevent any form of physical contact by remaining clothed; this maintains control over the sex. The fully clothed male will go from room to room, performing oral sex on as many men as possible. He remains dressed, keeping things as detached as possible. One person told me that a fully dressed man once rimmed him and sucked him for more than an hour. My friend tried to persuade him to take his clothes off, but he refused. The friend even tried to undress him physically, but he resisted, saying that sucking and rimming him was all he wanted to do.

Then there are the gay men who genuinely fear contracting a sexually transmitted infection (STI) or any other germs they believe are common in a bathhouse setting. These men desperately need sex but are genuinely paranoid about what lurks around the gay baths. When people think of a bathhouse, images of a dirty, scummy place come to mind. Staying dressed is a way for these men to protect themselves (they think) from all of the nasty bodily fluids that are circulating at the baths. I remember one person bringing brand-new garbage bags to store his clothes in a locker; that is how paranoid he was. But he is not the only one. It's common to observe numerous men walking the bathhouse hallways in their towels, wearing footwear. Most of these men are Asians because they're most paranoid about germs. Some even go further than that by wearing socks and shoes, which just look silly.

Then you have the men who start off fully clothed, only to end up undressed like everyone else. As I mentioned before, sometimes all a guy wants is a blowjob; hence, staying dressed. But during these interludes, some couples get so horny with each other that clothes start flying off. It can especially happen when a guy has just arrived at the baths. Before undressing, all gay men enjoy surveying the rooms upon arrival to see who is around. The same thing happens when guys put their clothes back on and prepare to leave the baths. They just want to have one more look around before departing.

Either way, a fully clothed guy might spot someone he likes and think, "Go for it. Why waste time undressing?" It is not uncommon to see a guy exit somebody's room practically naked, carrying a bunch of clothes with him. It happens more often than you think. I still remember eavesdropping on a couple in the room next to mine. It was summer, and I could hear one of the guys taking his clothes off and listening to him remove his shorts and underwear. The sound of his belt and keys jangling filled the air. You could hear the removal of a shirt, the kicking off of sandals, and the kissing. That was almost twenty years ago, and I still remember it as if it were yesterday.

I eagerly anticipate undressing when I arrive at the baths, as it instills in me a sense of liberation and tranquility. I love being completely naked, wrapped in my towel, and wearing nothing else, not even sandals. I tried wearing them, but they just made me feel clothed. I love the feeling of nakedness and wearing any footwear defeats that feeling.

Sometimes I forget that I am naked and surrounded by other nude men at the baths. That is how comfortable I have gotten with my nakedness. But being almost naked does have its drawbacks. Some guys I've met at the baths have picked up crabs (grabbing someone else's towel by mistake), fungus (from the steam room), and other viruses (like the flu). Those are all low-level but widespread bugs you can pick up when interacting with naked men at the baths.

In over twenty years of going to the baths, I have never picked up anything: no crabs, no foot fungus, no STI, nothing. I guess I must be under a lucky star.

Chapter 17
Sex Standing Up

If you want to be a regular patron at the baths, you must master one sexual activity in order to be a bathhouse pro. No, I'm not talking about being an experienced top or an oral expert. You need to know how to have sex while standing.

When you think of having sex, you think of this activity as horizontal, not vertical. However, this is not the case at the baths. This is primarily due to gay men's lack of interest in spending quality time. Nope, they want it fast, quick, and as many times as possible.

Consequently, you will witness men engaging in sexual activities while standing. Even if they have their own private room, guys think, "Why waste time? Let's do it now." Sex at the baths happens more often publicly than privately. Additionally, the baths offer numerous locations for intimate encounters—the sauna, the steam room, the hallway, the whirlpool, the shower area, the darkroom, and the list goes on.

Having sex in a vertical position is not as straightforward as it sounds. Maintaining balance while one hand holds your towel and the other simultaneously strokes your cock is a challenging task. Having sex with only one hand available is a challenge—but one you can learn with practice. Returning to the towel, my sole recommendation is to drape it around your neck. It can be awkward, as you want to press each other's chest skin-to-skin. Having this big fluffy towel around the neck gets in the way.

If you think that's difficult, try getting rimmed while standing. Your only recourse is to bend over and spread those legs. There's no position where you can elevate your legs while standing upright. Then there's the activity of performing oral sex in a squatting position. That makes juggling a towel even harder. But if you like to give blowjobs, you're in gay heaven at the baths. Given the abundance of available cocks, there are plenty of places to indulge in oral sex. It is truly a buyer's market. Plus, there are numerous glory holes to lurk around. However, since most of the guys will be standing, it's important to practice your squatting position. It is an excellent exercise for the muscles of the thighs, hips, and buttocks. This is an activity where you get two for the price of one!

What about trying to fuck someone? Why would anyone want to fuck standing when you can fuck horizontally on a bed in someone's room? Wouldn't that make more sense? Absolutely not, fucking someone against the wall is more of a turn-on than doing it on a bed. In addition, going to someone's room would mean the guy would give more of himself to the other person. He doesn't want to expose that intimate side of himself to just anyone. Sure, a guy can be hardcore and animalistic regarding sex. However, entering someone's room signifies a formal commitment to a specific person. Guys at the baths like to separate the personal from the sexual. Sex is sex. Period. My inner feelings are for myself, and I'm not giving them to you.

For instance, consider this man: he stands 6 feet tall, has blonde hair, blue eyes, and a well-defined physique. He can confidently enter any gay bar and attract any man, yet he consistently frequents the baths. He refuses to go into a guy's room or speak to anyone. He dresses in a bathing suit, goes into the darkroom, and stands there. He desires to have his body worshipped and sucked off. It is not uncommon for five men to be pawing him, sucking his nipples and cock, and running their hands over him all at once. However, he refrains from kissing, deeming it too intimate, and avoids exchanging words. He never goes after anyone; instead, he stands in a corner and waits for guys to come to him. He keeps his feet firmly planted on the ground to prevent anyone from removing his bathing suit. People have attempted to strip him completely naked. However, with his feet glued to the floor, that bathing suit always rests around his ankles.

Lack of a room is another factor contributing to the prevalence of sex while standing. Men will often hook up with another guy but discover neither has a room. Both only have lockers. This means that you need to find a place within the gay baths where you can engage in sexual activities. Fortunately, many baths have offered a solution to this problem. They have standing booths, similar to telephone booths, but without a telephone. Therefore, you and your partner enter the booth, close the door, and allow the magic to unfold. It is awkward and challenging to maneuver standing up. But what choice do you have? If you can't find privacy, it's booths or no sex.

If the bathhouse doesn't have privacy booths, you must have sex in the open. If you're an exhibitionist and don't mind guys watching, you're fine. But some are a bit shy about giving a blowjob in front of an audience. While most view the action from a distance, other guys can be pretty rude about how they watch.

Some men get up close when they watch guys having sex at the baths. How close? How about standing beside you, nose to nose, while he jerks off? These onlookers ignore any signals that this is private. They interpret public sex as an invitation to join in. It can be annoying to have uninvited men try to participate while you are enjoying yourself.

If you are an observer, here is the etiquette for this situation. If you see two men having sex and neither guy can pass as your twin, observe only.

Watch from a distance, and don't join in. But what if one of the men could pass for your twin? Follow the same advice as before but pay close attention to them. If you get a nod or a signal from either, slink over and join in.

Another reason to have sex standing up is to avoid breaking the mood by going back to someone's room. Everything is hot, and you're having fun. One of you suggests returning to his room, which you do. Upon arrival, there is no connection. Before, you were kissing and sucking, having a wonderful time. Now you discover that you're not sexually compatible—you're both bottoms, one dislikes rimming, or he is unattractive in the new light. There could be a variety of reasons for this, and going back to someone's room could change the vibe. So don't be surprised if your partner doesn't want to get horizontal in privacy. Either he wants it now, while standing, or he doesn't want to disrupt the mood. He has experienced one or the other, and it ended badly.

If you take anything from this essay about having sex vertically at the baths, follow this advice. Tall, lanky guys make the best lovers to have sex with standing up.

Chapter 18
Gay Quickies

One thing synonymous with a bathhouse is quickie sex, which takes place on an hourly basis. You would think that gay men would want to spend as much time as possible enjoying sex. However, many guys have told me that they prefer quickies because they are exactly that: They are concise and direct. There is no intimacy, no getting to know the other person, or any type of emotional bonding. Guys would rather save those feelings of pure lovemaking for someone they genuinely like.

That is one of the reasons why many men do not purchase a room when they visit the baths. Getting a room means subconsciously preparing for the possibility of spending quality time with another person. By getting a locker, you are categorizing sex as frequent and easy, with little hassle. You exchange no contact information, don't know each other's names, and don't need to show courtesy. You view each other as objects with the sole purpose of enjoying each other's bodies. Getting a locker also gives you an "out." Without a room, guys have no choice but to hook up openly. Because of that, it is easier to walk away from a sexual interlude that goes nowhere. If the same thing happens with two guys in a room, it is harder to kick someone out without being blunt or rude. That's how the baths operate: they involve quick, straightforward sex.

Many men have told me that they even refrain from kissing other guys. Oral sex—no problem. Anal: pass the lube. But kissing? NO WAY! You would think it would be the other way around. I have always equated oral sex as a personal, intimate bonding experience between two people who genuinely care for one another. It's the opportunity to let go and give yourself to the other person. However, I must remove myself from the heterosexual perspective. In the homosexual world, the situation is reversed. In the gay world, kissing is equivalent to displaying intimate affection— between two guys who genuinely love each other. Whether it's oral or anal, you can experience it around the clock. Men want to save their actual, physical, close contact for a future boyfriend.

However, let us face reality. Because finding a partner or boyfriend is complex, many guys remain single for years between relationships. How many gay couples do you know that have lasted over a year? Therefore, quickie sex becomes a way to escape from that never-ending quest to find Mr. Right. That's why baths are the perfect place to satisfy your sexual craving fast. You save so much time at the baths compared to trolling through a hookup app. Scrolling through an online list of available guys is equivalent to the time it takes to arrive at the baths, get laid, and then return home.

Many guys are just looking for a quick blowjob or anal. They don't care about the location of the sex as long as it's brief and direct. I recall a businessman who arrived immaculately dressed. He stripped off his clothes, went to someone's room, took a shower, got dressed, and then left. This entire process took only 20 minutes! You would think that when a man enters the baths with six hours to spare, he will spend all six hours with a guy he's just met. However, the issue lies in the intimacy factor. Men often avoid getting close to a guy unless there is a developing relationship. Gay men view the gay baths as a means to ejaculate until their next encounter. That is what 's so great about the baths. Sex is easily accessible and direct. It is common for guys to have three to five quickies in an hour! Men can spend as little as ten minutes at the gay baths. However, diversity is indeed the essence of life. Having sex out in the open is bound to attract a crowd. However, if you see two men going at it in public,

Can you stay and watch?

Can you join them?

Just what is the etiquette?

Here's the etiquette to watch and join in.

What is the protocol to observe? How do you handle it? If I am in the sauna or steam room and two guys suddenly come in and start making out, I can stay and watch. I arrived first, so if they had a problem, they wouldn't have come in. However, if the couple had entered the sauna or steam room before me and began engaging in sexual activities,

I would refrain from entering and would stay away. You don't know how comfortable they are with people watching. Most of the time, men find it uncomfortable when others watch them engage in sexual activity. If a couple feels like too many eyes are watching, they will leave to find a private area.

Regrettably, certain individuals at the baths will follow a couple who are attempting to have a quickie. These men will follow the couple from room to room, wanting to "watch." That is poor bathhouse etiquette. However, some couples are pure exhibitionists, having no problem with an audience. Therefore, if a crowd watches two guys going at it, you can observe. Let's face it: This is a live sex show, complete with full-on hard-ons. How often do you see that? Porn movies notwithstanding.

But could you join in and make it a threesome instead of watching? It does happen that other men will join in, making it a threesome or even a foursome. But what is the etiquette for joining in? It depends on the situation. If you see two guys getting it on, wait for a signal from them that you can participate. A wink, a nod, or even a hand wave will give you an indication. If you don't see any of these signs, they may be uninterested in a third party. If you attempt to join in without a sign, you may face pushback. This can happen either gently or with great force. That is embarrassing, so wait for the signals. If you do not care about being shot down, go for it. However, be aware that physical pushing may serve as a warning to retreat. Again, you cannot take this rejection personally; that is how the baths are.

Now that you understand the proper etiquette for witnessing and participating in group sex, let's explore the areas in a bathhouse where these intimate moments can take place: The wet area, which includes the sauna, steam, whirlpool, and shower; the porn lounge; and lastly, the orgy room are the areas where these quickies can transpire in a bathhouse.

The Wet Area

It's an area where men eventually converge during their travels inside a bathhouse. This section usually has showers, a whirlpool, a sauna or steam room, a sink and mirrors, and a toilet. Men often congregate in the wet area, cruising and seeking their next sexual encounter. Eventually, many guys cruising a bathhouse's hallways will wind up in the sauna or steam room.

Sauna or Steam Room

Quickie encounters between two guys in the sauna will happen one of two ways. By chance, two men end up there. Alternatively, one individual pursues the other into the sauna. As the two men sit together in the sauna, they establish eye contact to gauge any potential interest.

If there is interest, one of the men will start to stroke until he achieves a full erection. If the other guy is not interested, he will leave. But if he stays, the next step is to touch each other's erections. Finally, they suck each other off. These quickies in a sauna usually last ten to fifteen minutes. Because of the heat inside the sauna, fresh air is necessary to breathe, so these sauna quickies don't last long. Couples must leave the steam to continue their liaison elsewhere in the baths. But some guys have incredible staying power, going on for over an hour in the heat!

Whirlpool

A quickie in a whirlpool presents its own unique set of circumstances. I have a friend named Mike who visits the bathhouse strictly for relaxation. I don't think he cares if he gets off, as Mike spends almost all his time in the pool. But what if a charming guy dips in? Mike will make the first move. First, he positions himself, so he is opposite or near the guy. Then Mike "accidentally" brushes his leg against the other guy. If he does not respond or moves away, then Mike knows the other guy is uninterested. But if the guy returns the "accidental brush" with his own feet, then Mike starts to reel him in. Initially, Mike engages in footsies with the other man, raising his foot to a level where he can massage the other guy's genitalia. These two guys will soon feel each other up with some oral and simulating anal—all within a 15-minute encounter in the whirlpool. Most likely, an audience will gather to observe this whirlpool encounter. Due to the intense heat, the man will likely exit the whirlpool and walk away. Neither man has ejaculated. Mike usually stays in the pool, relaxing and enjoying the waves. Mike is satisfied for the time being, until the next guy enters the whirlpool.

Shower Area

The baths' shower areas are popular for quickie sex. Similar to the sauna area, guys enjoy cruising each other while taking a shower. In an effort to attract attention, guys will start off by soaping up their cock until achieving a full erection. Some men skip soaping up their dick in order to be more direct. Reaching out to touch the other guy's cock is another tactic. If the other guy is uninterested, he will say, "No thanks," and walk away. But if the other guy is interested, he will reciprocate. Soon the two guys begin caressing and soaping each other, sliding their wet, soapy bodies together. Soon, one of the guys will start sucking the other guy off. Both showerheads are still running full blast, with steaming hot water falling on both men.

Guys hook up in the wet area more often than you might think. Couples face a problem with how open the wet area is. There is no privacy, so naturally, couples leave the wet area to escape the stares and crowds. Unfortunately, if neither man has a room, they have one of three choices. First, one of the guys can exchange their locker for a room. Secondly, they can both change into new clothes and inquire, "Your place or mine?" Third, they can find a more discreet place in the bathhouse, usually the porn lounge or the orgy room. Both of those rooms are where most quickies typically take place.

Porn Lounge

The porn lounge is sort of like the sauna. It is the one room where I have seen the wildest action. Over the years, I have seen my share of rimming, oral, threesomes, and foursomes in the porn lounge. The main difference between the sauna and the porn lounge is that you can see gay porn images onscreen. Simultaneously, you can witness men stroking themselves to ejaculate as they watch gay porn. The porn lounge is the one area of the baths that elicits the quickest sex. Like in a sauna, if two guys find each other hot while stroking themselves to full erections, they will go for it. In front of an audience, they engage in kissing, suckling, and rimming each other with fully erect cocks.

Oftentimes, having so many people watching them can make a couple feel uncomfortable. They put a chair in front of them (as if that would help). Most times, a couple leaves to find a dark corner in a hallway or even an unoccupied restroom stall.

At one point, I entered the porn lounge and was taken aback by the sight of two men engaging in raw anal sex. The two men assumed the following positions: Guy A was sitting, and Guy B was sitting on him, pumping up and down. After a few minutes, Guy A grabbed Guy B, lifted him, positioned him on all fours (doggy style), and started to pump him again, thrusting his cock in and out. After another few minutes, they changed positions; Guy B was lying on his back, with Guy A continuing to pump his cock in and out. After another few minutes, Guy B got up, leaned against the wall, and had Guy A pump him out of that position. After that, they seemed worn out and stopped. Neither man came, nor were condoms used. They chitchatted for a bit, with Guy A saying he could go for hours without ejaculating. Guy B expressed his gratitude and continued his journey.

Dark Room

The last place you can get quickie sex in a bathhouse is the darkroom (or the orgy room). This room also serves couples looking for privacy (when both parties only have a locker).

Many couples enjoy having sex openly in a dark room, on a bench, or in slings. They relish having men stare at them while having sex. These are the guys who like to be voyeurs.

The darkness envelopes you as soon as you enter the darkroom. You can hardly make out what other guys are doing. You have to wait for your eyes to adjust to the darkness. But once your eyes change, you see shadows and bodies moving, giving couples some privacy. Most times you stand there and watch others have sex in the darkness.

These rooms can feature everything from open booths (like a telephone booth so you can have privacy), multiple Glory Holes for group play, and other dark (or pitch-dark) spaces with some benches (in case two guys want to do anal).

Years ago, an episode of "Queer as Folk" showed an orgy room inside a bathhouse. When that episode hit the airwaves, I received dozens of requests from men asking me to recommend a bathhouse in their city. The scenes featured dozens of men all having sex with one another, oblivious to who was watching. In my opinion, that scene is pure fiction. In the twenty-plus years that I have gone to the baths, I have never seen multiple orgies. I might have seen a foursome once or twice, but that was it. I say it is fiction because group sex is supposed to be an unbridled passion where guys just go for it, regardless of the other person's appearance.

In theory, that is what group sex should be. However, gay men have preferences. For group sex to be successful, everyone in the group must feel attracted to each other. That doesn't happen. It is possible for one person to find only certain individuals attractive. Simultaneously, someone else might find only one individual attractive. So instead of this big 20-person session, you have different groups of three or four going at it. You may switch between groups, but in reality, it is five separate groups rather than a single group of 20. For one big sex group to function, all 20 people must find each other attractive. It's impossible to arrange a spontaneous 20-person sex session at the baths without prior planning. When group sex occurs in these dark rooms, it signifies a desperation for sexual activity that compels all participants to blindly pursue unknown individuals. However, if someone were to suddenly turn on the lights in a dark room during a 20-person group session, the session would immediately break up due to superficial bias.

With so many men available in a bathhouse for a 15-minute "quickie," you might ask yourself, "Where are the men who like to cuddle?" That's my favorite form of sex, just between you and me.

Please stay tuned for my next story, where I will demonstrate the concept of "Real Men Cuddle."

My second book, "Back To The Baths: More Gay Bathhouse Stories"

.

CONTACT BATHHOUSE BLUES

website - bathhouseblues.com

twitter - @bathhouseblues

9 798227 671035